This book belongs to

D1338810

....

The Bigfoot Mystery
and Other Stories

How this collection works

This *Biff, Chip and Kipper* collection is one of a series of four books at **Read with Oxford Stage 4**. It contains four stories: *On the Stage*, *The Bigfoot Mystery*, *Magic Tricks* and *Holiday in Japan*. These stories will help to broaden your child's wider reading experience. There are also fun activities to enjoy throughout the book.

How to use this book

Find a time to read with your child when they are not too tired and are happy to concentrate for about fifteen to twenty minutes. Reading with your child should be a shared and enjoyable experience. It is best to choose just one of the stories for each session.

For each story, there are tips for reading the story together. At the end of the story you will find four 'Talk about the story' questions. These will help your child to think about what they have read, and to relate the story to their own experiences. The questions are followed by a fun activity.

Enjoy sharing the stories!

Contents

OXFORD
UNIVERSITY PRESS

Authors and illustrators

On the Stage written by Roderick Hunt, illustrated by Nick Schon

The Bigfoot Mystery written by Paul Shipton, illustrated by Nick Schon

Magic Tricks written by Paul Shipton, illustrated by Nick Schon

Holiday in Japan written by Roderick Hunt, illustrated by Alex Brychta

OXFORD
UNIVERSITY PRESS

Great Clarendon Street, Oxford, OX2 6DP, United Kingdom

Oxford University Press is a department of the University
of Oxford. It furthers the University's objective of excellence
in research, scholarship, and education by publishing
worldwide. Oxford is a registered trade mark of Oxford
University Press in the UK and in certain other countries

On the Stage, *Holiday in Japan* text © Roderick Hunt 2015
The Bigfoot Mystery, *Magic Tricks* text by Paul Shipton © Oxford University Press 2015

Holiday in Japan illustrations © Alex Brychta 2015
On the Stage, *The Bigfoot Mystery*, *Magic Tricks* illustrations by Nick Schon © Oxford University Press 2015

The characters in this work are the original creation of Roderick Hunt
and Alex Brychta who retain copyright in the characters

The moral rights of the authors have been asserted

On the Stage, *The Bigfoot Mystery*, *Magic Tricks*, *Holiday in Japan* first published in 2015
This Edition published in 2018

British Library Cataloguing in Publication Data
Data available

ISBN: 978-0-19-276428-7

10 9 8 7 6

Paper used in the production of this book is a natural, recyclable product
made from wood grown in sustainable forests. The manufacturing process
conforms to the environmental regulations of the country of origin.

Printed in Great Britain by Bell and Bain Ltd, Glasgow

MIX
Paper from
responsible sources
FSC® C007785

Acknowledgements

Series Editor: Annemarie Young
Additional artwork by Stuart Trotter
p132: Japan and New Zealand maps by Shutterstock

Tips for reading *On the Stage*

Children learn best when reading is relaxed and enjoyable.

- Talk about the title and the picture on page 6. Then read the speech bubble.

- Discuss what you think the story might be about.

- Share the story, encouraging your child to read as much of it as they can.

- Give lots of praise as your child reads, and help them when necessary.

- If your child gets stuck on a word that is decodable, encourage them to say the sounds and then blend them together to read the word. Read the whole sentence again. Focus on the meaning.

- If the word is not decodable, or is still too tricky, just read the word for them, re-read the sentence and move on.

- When you've finished reading the story, talk about it with your child, using the 'Talk about the story' questions at the end. Then do the activity.

Children enjoy re-reading stories, and this helps to build their confidence.

Have fun!

For more activities, free eBooks and practical advice to help your child progress with reading visit **oxfordowl.co.uk**

On the Stage

A show about the Wild West leads to an adventure on a stagecoach!

Wilma, Wilf and Biff were in a show about the
Wild West. They wore jeans and cowboy boots.
Wilma's skirt had a fringe along the edge.

They had to sing a song about a stagecoach
coming into town. It was hard to get it right and
they had to stay late to practise.

Mum had lent Biff her mobile phone. Biff rang her when it was time to go.

"Mum is going to pick us all up," she told Wilf and Wilma.

Wilf and Wilma went home with Biff.

"Come and play in my room until your Dad comes to pick you up," said Biff.

Biff still had Mum's mobile phone.

"I wish I had a mobile," said Wilma.

Then the magic key began to glow.

The magic took them to the Wild West.

"The desert!" said Wilma. "What an amazing place in the world to be."

A stagecoach was racing along the desert trail.
It was pulled by four horses. Dust flew up round
the horses' hooves.

The stagecoach pulled up when it saw the children.
"Slow down! Take care!" the driver shouted at
the horses.

The driver looked at the children with astonishment.

"What are you kids doing out here in the desert?" he gasped.

"Er . . . we are lost," said Wilf.

"I'll take you to the next town," said the driver, "and hand you to the sheriff."

The children sat on a seat on top of the stagecoach.

"No seat belts," shouted Biff. "Take care! Hang on!"

The edge of the trail was bumpy and cracked.
The stagecoach began to rock. The wheels ran into
a deep crack in the ground.

The horses bucked. The driver pulled the reins.
Then the wheels sank deeper into the crack and the
stagecoach stopped with a jerk.

"It won't budge," said the driver. "The town is still
a long way off. We can't get help until tomorrow."

Biff saw smoke in the distance.

"It must be from the new railroad," said a man.

"They are even laying railway track across the desert."

"Use the mobile phone," said Wilf.

"That's no good," said Biff. "Mobile phones aren't invented here, yet."

"No! Use it like a mirror," said Wilf.

"The screen will flash and reflect the sun," Wilf
went on.

"Good thinking," said Biff. "People in the
distance might see it flashing."

Over on the new railroad, the boss was looking through a telescope.

"Someone's in trouble," he said. "It looks like the stagecoach."

A gang of men rode across from the railroad. They looked at the stagecoach and said they would go and get levers and ropes.

"Flashing that bright mirror was clever," said
the boss.

It took a long time but, in the end, the men
lifted the stagecoach out.

The stagecoach set off again.

"Well, we won't need a stagecoach when the railroad is finished," said the boss.

In town, the driver called, "Now I'm going to take you to the sheriff."

But the magic key had already glowed and the children had gone.

The children went back to Biff's room.

"What an adventure!" said Wilf. "Now we know what a real stagecoach was like."

In the show everyone loved the song about
the stagecoach.

"They've never sung it better," said Mum.

Talk about the story

How did the stagecoach get stuck?

How did Biff's mobile phone help them?

Why do you think the stagecoach won't be needed once the railroad is finished?

What's your favourite way of travelling?

Decode the message

Here is another way to send a message. It is called semaphore.

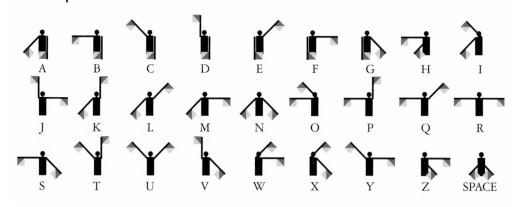

A B C D E F G H I
J K L M N O P Q R
S T U V W X Y Z SPACE

What message is Biff sending?

S G N D SPACE H E

Tips for reading *The Bigfoot Mystery*

Children learn best when reading is relaxed and enjoyable.

- Talk about the title and the picture on page 34. Then read the speech bubble.

- Discuss what you think the story might be about.

- Share the story, encouraging your child to read as much of it as they can.

- Give lots of praise as your child reads, and help them when necessary.

- If your child gets stuck on a word that is decodable, encourage them to say the sounds and then blend them together to read the word. Read the whole sentence again. Focus on the meaning.

- If the word is not decodable, or is still too tricky, just read the word for them, re-read the sentence and move on.

- When you've finished reading the story, talk about it with your child, using the 'Talk about the story' questions at the end. Then do the activity.

Children enjoy re-reading stories, and this helps to build their confidence.

Have fun!

 For more activities, free eBooks and practical advice to help your child progress with reading visit **oxfordowl.co.uk**

The Bigfoot Mystery

The magic key takes the children to a forest. What mystery animal do they meet?

Mum was checking Kipper's <u>trainers</u>.

"Are these your toes at the end?" she asked.

"Your feet have grown again!"

"You need a new pair of trainers," said
Mum. "Go and tell Biff and Chip that we're going
to the shops."

    As soon as Kipper peeked into Biff's room, the
magic key started to glow.

    It was time for an adventure.

The magic took them to a forest with lots of
tall trees.

Biff saw a footprint in the mud.

"Look at this," she said. "It's enormous!"

She put her own foot next to the footprint
to compare.

"What made it?" asked Kipper. "A bear?"

"Bears have paws with sharp claws," said Biff.
"This footprint has toe marks."

"Some people believe a mystery animal called
Bigfoot lives in the woods," said Chip.

"Perhaps Bigfoot made the footprint," Chip added.

"Here is another mystery," said Kipper. "Why is this rope here?"

Biff and Chip went to check.

Suddenly a big, wooden cage dropped down over the three children.

"Oh no!" shouted Chip. "It's a trap!"

The children tried to lift up the cage but it was
much too heavy.

"Help!" shouted Kipper. "Is anybody there?"

"Yes!" said Biff. "Look over there."

A huge, hairy creature was watching them. It looked interested.

"That's Bigfoot!" said Chip in amazement.

Bigfoot came closer.

"I think he wants to help us," said Biff.

The <u>wooden</u> cage was not heavy for Bigfoot. He
lifted it off the children easily.

"We're free!" said Chip.

Biff looked up at Bigfoot. "Thanks for helping us," she said.

Bigfoot seemed to smile at the children.

Suddenly they heard gruff voices.

"The trap is this way," said a man.

Bigfoot looked round. Now he seemed frightened.

He ran into the woods and hid.

A moment later three men appeared.

"What are you children doing here?" one of them asked.

"We're lost," said Chip quickly.

"My name is Mr Bunkum," said the man.
"We set that trap to catch a mystery animal
called Bigfoot."

Bigfoot stayed hidden and watched.

"What will you do if you catch him?" Biff asked Bunkum.

Bunkum smiled. "I'm going to take him all
around the world in my travelling circus. People will
pay lots of money to see him. He is the only Bigfoot
in the world!"

Bunkum gave the children a hard stare.

"Have you seen Bigfoot near here?" he asked.

The children did not think Bunkum's plan sounded very nice for Bigfoot.

Biff, Chip and Kipper looked at each other. They shook their heads.

Chip quietly rubbed his foot over the footprint so the men would not see it.

"Maybe I'll go and look for the Loch Ness monster instead!" Bunkum said crossly.

The magic key began to glow.

"What's that? A magic key!" shouted Bunkum.

"People will pay lots to see that!"

The children started <u>disappearing</u>.

"Come back!" Bunkum shouted <u>angrily</u>.

He did not know that Bigfoot was behind him,
waving goodbye to the children.

At home Mum was waiting to take Kipper
shopping for new trainers.

"Go on then, Bigfoot," joked Biff to her little
brother.

Talk about the story

Why did Biff say the footprint couldn't have been made by a bear?

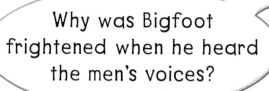

Why was Bigfoot frightened when he heard the men's voices?

Why did Mr Bunkum give the children a hard stare?

What would you do if you found an animal in trouble?

Word games

Make nine compound words from the words below. For
example: fire + ball = fireball

man

foot

flower

ball

pot

print

fire

ball

shine

sun

brow

eye

Tips for reading *Magic Tricks*

Children learn best when reading is relaxed and enjoyable.

- Talk about the title and the picture on page 62. Then read the speech bubble.

- Discuss what you think the story might be about.

- Share the story, encouraging your child to read as much of it as they can.

- Give lots of praise as your child reads, and help them when necessary.

- If your child gets stuck on a word that is decodable, encourage them to say the sounds and then blend them together to read the word. Read the whole sentence again. Focus on the meaning.

- If the word is not decodable, or is still too tricky, just read the word for them, re-read the sentence and move on.

- When you've finished reading the story, talk about it with your child, using the 'Talk about the story' questions at the end. Then do the activity.

Children enjoy re-reading stories, and this helps to build their confidence.

Have fun!

For more activities, free eBooks and practical advice to help your child progress with reading visit **oxfordowl.co.uk**

Magic Tricks

Can Wilf fool a magician with his magic trick?

"Let's play cards," said Chip.

Wilf wanted to show his friends a new magic trick instead. He took a pack of cards from his pocket.

"Pick a card," he said to Biff.

"Don't show me your card," said Wilf.

He closed his eyes and put his fingers on his forehead.

"Is your card the eight of clubs?" he asked.

"It is!" said Biff. "Wow!"

Wilf showed them the other cards. "It's a special pack from my new magic set," he said. "All of the cards are the same!"

"That's a great trick, Wilf," said Chip.
At that moment the magic key began to glow.

"I wonder where the magic is going to take us now," said Biff.

"I don't know," said Wilf. "But I'm going to take my trick cards!"

The magic took them to the entrance of a fancy
old theatre.

"Why has the magic key brought us here?"
asked Chip.

Biff pointed to a poster on the wall.

The poster was for 'Marvo the Magnificent'.
"It says that he is the greatest magician
in the whole wide world!" said Wilf. "I wish we
could see him!"

"You *can* see him," said a tall man behind the children. "Marvo the Magnificent's show is starting in a few moments." He pointed towards a door into the theatre.

"We haven't got tickets," said Biff.

The tall man smiled and clicked his fingers.
Suddenly there were three tickets in his hands. "For
you," he said.

"Wow!" said Wilf. "Thanks!"

There were lots of people in the theatre, but the
children found three empty seats near the stage.

As soon as they sat down, the lights went dim.

"Ladies and gentlemen," said a voice in the
dark. "Put your hands together for the incredible
. . . the amazing . . . Marvo the Magnificent!"
The audience all began to clap.

"It's the man we saw before!" said Wilf. "*He's*
Marvo the Magnificent!"

Marvo lifted his top hat and gave a bow to
the audience.

"Prepare to be amazed and astounded," Marvo said with a smile.

There was a flash of light and a bird flew out of his top hat.

"Wow!" said Wilf.

Marvo had been right. His magic tricks *were* amazing and astounding. After every trick, the children asked each other, "How did he do *that*?"

"For my next trick," said Marvo, "I need a
volunteer from the audience."

Lots of people in the crowd put up their hands,
but Marvo pointed right at Biff.

When Biff came on stage, Marvo said, "Please
tell us what is in your pocket."

"A key," said Biff. She put one hand into her
pocket, but there was no key.

"Are you looking for this?" asked Marvo with a smile.

There was a puff of smoke as Marvo pulled something from the top hat.

"The key!" said Biff in surprise.

The audience clapped and cheered.

Marvo gave another bow and said, "Thank you, ladies and gentlemen, and goodnight."

Then he walked quickly off the stage.

"That was fantastic!" said Wilf. "I wish I could do magic tricks like that!"

"It *was* good," agreed Chip. "But why isn't the magic key taking us home now?"

Biff pulled out the key from her pocket and stared at it.

"Wait a minute," she said. "There's something different about this key. It isn't the magic key!"

"Marvo must have heard us talking about the magic key," said Chip. "He gave us the tickets because he was planning to get it. He swapped the keys when you were on stage!"

"We can't go home without the magic key," said
Chip unhappily.

"Don't worry," said Biff. "We're going to find
Marvo and get our key back. Come on!"

They found Marvo the Magnificent sitting in a little dressing room behind the stage.

"You tricked us," said Biff crossly. "Now we want our key back."

Marvo did not give them the key.

"The world's only magic key should be *mine*,"
he said. "I am the greatest magician in the world,
after all. It says so on my poster!"

Wilf could feel the pack of cards in his pocket.

"What if I can fool you with a magic trick?" he said. "Then will you give us the key?"

Marvo just smiled. "*If* you can fool me, of course
I will give you the key. But you *won't* be able to
fool me. I am Marvo the Magnificent!"

Wilf took the cards out of his pocket.

"Pick a card," he told Marvo.

With a confident grin, Marvo pulled one card from the pack.

"Is your card the eight of clubs?" Wilf asked him.

"Of course it is!" said Marvo. "But that trick didn't fool me. *Every* card in that pack is the same. Let me see!"

Marvo plucked the pack of cards from Wilf's hands.

The magician turned the cards over. Then he gasped in surprise. All of the cards were different. "But how?" he asked.

Wilf did not know either. He was just as surprised.

"Now where's our key?" asked Biff.

Before Marvo could answer, the key started glowing inside the top hat. Biff grabbed it. "Goodbye, Marvo the *not* so Magnificent!" she said.

At home Wilf said, "I see what happened. I must
have picked up your cards instead of my trick pack."

"So how did you guess Marvo's card correctly?"
asked Chip.

"Maybe I was just *really* lucky," said Wilf.

"Or maybe the key helped you," suggested Biff.

Wilf looked at the key. "Wow," he said. "Now *that's* magic!"

Talk about the story

Why did Marvo the magician give the children free tickets to his performance?

How did Marvo get the magic key from Biff?

What do you think Marvo would do with the magic key?

What sort of magic tricks would you like to do?

Create words

Magic up some words!

Make some new words by adding the red or green letters
to the blue words.

hope

re-

happy

-less

rest

white

un-

pack

-ness

fit

-ful

Tips for reading *Holiday in Japan*

Children learn best when reading is relaxed and enjoyable.

- Talk about the title and the picture on page 98. Then read the speech bubble.
- Discuss what you think the story might be about.
- Share the story, encouraging your child to read as much of it as they can.
- Give lots of praise as your child reads, and help them when necessary.
- If your child gets stuck on a word that is decodable, encourage them to say the sounds and then blend them together to read the word. Read the whole sentence again. Focus on the meaning.
- If the word is not decodable, or is still too tricky, just read the word for them, re-read the sentence and move on.
- When you've finished reading the story, talk about it with your child, using the 'Talk about the story' questions at the end. Then do the activity.

Children enjoy re-reading stories, and this helps to build their confidence.

Have fun!

For more activities, free eBooks and practical advice to help your child progress with reading visit **oxfordowl.co.uk**

Holiday in Japan

Dad had gone to London for an important meeting. He called Mum and sounded very excited. "Guess where I am going?" he said. "To Japan."

"Dad's going to Japan," Kipper told Gran. "A company in Tokyo wants to use the machine that Dad's company has invented. Dad has to show it to them."

"Gran knows," said Dad.

"I do," said Gran. "I've had a good idea. I'll pay for you *all* to fly to Tokyo."

"Wow!" said Biff. "Thank you! You are the best gran in the world."

It was a long flight to Tokyo. It took over
twelve hours.

"It's halfway round the world," said Biff.

"I'll be glad to get there," said Mum "You've all
slept, but I haven't."

Mr Yamada met them at the airport. His wife
Yoko and daughter Rio were with him.

"We are glad the children came with you," said
Mr Yamada.

"Welcome to Japan," said Rio shyly.

"Rio is learning English," said Yoko.

"You look really pretty, Rio," said Mum. "Is your dress called a kimono?"

"It's my summer kimono," said Rio. "It's called a yukata."

"Now let's go to your hotel," said Mr Yamada. "Tokyo is a very busy city. It will take us about an hour to get there."

They were amazed when they saw the hotel.
It was very tall.

"Your rooms are near the top," said Mr Yamada.
"Tomorrow, Yoko and Rio will be happy to take
you sightseeing."

Biff and Chip took pictures of their hotel bedroom and sent them to Gran.

"It's an amazing room," said Chip. "We can see for miles across the city."

The next day, Yoko and Rio took Mum and the children sightseeing. The streets were very busy.

"Stay close to us," said Yoko. "You don't want to get lost."

They came to a huge toy store.

"Oh wow!" said Kipper. "Can we go in?"

"Not now," laughed Yoko. "It has five floors.
We'd never get you out!"

They went to see a beautiful temple.

"It is the oldest temple in Tokyo," said Yoko.

"It's lovely," said Chip.

Paper lanterns hung at the entrance. People
stood in front of the temple to pray.

"Who are the men in robes?" asked Kipper.

"They are monks," said Yoko.

There were little shops near the temple.

"Look at these lovely fans," said Biff. "Let's buy one for Gran."

"That's a good idea," said Mum.

"It's time for lunch," said Yoko. "These are called bento boxes. Do you think you can use chopsticks?"

"The food looks such fun," said Kipper, "and I'll try to eat with chopsticks."

At last it was time to go back to the hotel. But on the way to the station, they lost Yoko and Rio.

"Oh dear," said Mum. "We had better try and find the station by ourselves."

"Which way do we go?" said Mum.

At that moment, some school children stopped.

They were excited about Kipper's fair hair.

"Do you speak English?" asked Kipper.

"Is it this way or that way?" said Mum.

"Don't worry, Mum," said Kipper. "My new friends will take us to the station."

"We use the train every day," they said.

They found Yoko and Rio at the station.

"Thank goodness you found your way here," said Yoko.

"Thanks to my new friends. I'm going to write to them when I get home," said Kipper.

The next day, the family set off on the bullet train to go to Kyoto. Rio and her parents came to see them off.

"Wow! Look at the train," said Biff. "It goes at 300 kilometres an hour."

On the train, the conductor inspected tickets.
When she got to the children she smiled and pointed
out of the window.

"You are lucky today!" she said.

Biff looked out and gasped.

In the distance was Mount Fuji.

"We *are* lucky," said Dad. "It's a clear day. It's not often you can see it."

The mountain was capped with snow.

"It's an amazing shape," said Biff.

"It is an active volcano," said Dad. "That's why it is that shape."

"It won't erupt, will it?" asked Chip.

"The last time was in 1708," said Dad, "so I don't think so."

In Kyoto, the hotel was different. It was a traditional
Japanese inn.

"I love the bedroom," said Biff. "It is so different from
the other hotel. We must take lots of pictures to show Gran."

"We are going to sleep on these mats, called tatami mats," said Dad.

"But on mattresses," said Mum. "And there's a wooden bath. It's to soak in. You must shower before you use it."

It was time to explore Kyoto.

"Kyoto used to be the capital city of Japan,"
said Dad. "One of its most beautiful buildings is
the Golden Pavilion."

"Oh wow! It really is beautiful. Can we go inside?"
asked Kipper.

"I don't know," said Mum.

A lady with a dog heard what Mum had said.

"It is not possible to go inside," she said.

"Do you know that it is covered in real gold?"

In a part of the garden was a pot. The kind
lady told them it was lucky to throw coins in it.

"May you always have good luck," she said.

At last it was time to fly home.

"I'll never forget our holiday in Japan," said Kipper.

"We *are* lucky to have seen all those places in Tokyo and Kyoto," said Biff.

Gran met them at the airport.

"We have had a wonderful holiday," said Biff. "We can't wait to tell you all about it. Thank you so much, Gran."

The children spoke to Rio online.

"We still remember the Japanese you taught us,
Rio," said Chip.

"Arigato – thank you!" Biff, Chip and Kipper
all said together.

Talk about the story

Why did the flight to Japan take so long?

Why did the school children stop when they saw Kipper?

Why did the train conductor say they were lucky?

Where would you like to visit on holiday?

Word search

Find the seven country names below.

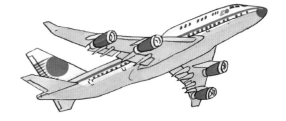

Germany Russia Greece Japan
India Canada Peru

K R E N J C W O

G I N D I A Y F

R W D V Z N C D

E U B G A A R P

E D S M O D H U

C K R S J A R I

E E L M I E O P

G R J A P A N Q

Remembering the stories together

Encourage your child to remember and retell the stories in this book. You could ask questions like these:

- Who are the characters in the story?
- What happens at the beginning of the story?
- What happens next?
- How does the story end?
- What was your favourite part of the story? Why?

Story prompts

When talking to your child about the stories, you could use these more detailed reminders to help them remember the exact sequence of events. Turn the statements below into questions, so that your child can give you the answers. For example, *Where does the magic key take the children? What happens to the stagecoach and who helps?* And so on …

On the Stage

- After the children put on a show about the Wild West, the magic key takes them on an adventure.
- Their stagecoach gets stuck and Biff uses her phone to get help.
- Some men see Biff's phone signal and come to help them.
- The men fix the problem and the magic key takes the children home.

The Bigfoot Mystery

- Kipper needs new shoes, but before they can go shopping, the magic key takes them on an adventure.
- The children are taken to a forest where they find a big footprint on the ground.
- They get caught in a trap and Bigfoot comes to their rescue!

- Some men come looking for Bigfoot.
- The children protect Bigfoot from the men. The key takes them home.

Magic tricks

- The children like playing card tricks.
- The magic key takes them to an old theatre where a magician is performing.
- They are given tickets to watch the show.
- They are amazed by all the tricks and Biff is called up on stage to take part.

- The magician somehow gets the magic key from Biff's pocket and swaps it for a different key!
- Wilf manages to trick the magician into giving back the magic key and they can head home.

Holiday in Japan

- Dad has to go to Japan on business and Gran pays for the family to go with him.
- They go sightseeing in Tokyo with Yoko and Rio, their new Japanese friends.
- Yoko teaches the children how to use chopsticks.
- They get lost, but some schoolchildren help them.

- The next day, they go on a very fast train, see Mount Fuji and stay in a traditional Japanese hotel.
- When they get back home, they keep in touch with Rio online.

You could now encourage your child to create a 'story map' of each story, drawing and colouring all the key parts of them. This will help them identify the main elements of the stories and learn to create their own stories.